TABLE OF CONTENTS

Novel-Ties® are printed on recycled paper.

Copyright © 1999, 2006, 2013 by LEARNING LINKS

For the Teacher

This reproducible study guide to use in conjunction with the book *Frindle* consists of lessons for guided reading. Written in chapter-by-chapter format, the guide contains a synopsis, pre-reading activities, vocabulary and comprehension exercises, as well as extension activities to be used as follow-up to the novel.

In a homogeneous classroom, whole class instruction with one title is appropriate. In a heterogeneous classroom, reading groups should be formed: each group works on a different novel at its own reading level. Depending upon the length of time devoted to reading in the classroom, each novel, with its guide and accompanying lessons, may be completed in three to six weeks.

Begin using NOVEL-TIES for reading development by distributing the novel and a folder to each child. Distribute duplicated pages of the study guide for students to place in their folders. After examining the cover and glancing through the book, students can participate in several pre-reading activities. Vocabulary questions should be considered prior to reading a chapter; all other work should be done after the chapter has been read. Comprehension questions can be answered orally or in writing. The classroom teacher should determine the amount of work to be assigned, always keeping in mind that readers must be nurtured and that the ultimate goal is encouraging students' love of reading.

The benefits of using NOVEL-TIES are numerous. Students read good literature in the original, rather than in abridged or edited form. The good reading habits, formed by practice in focusing on interpretive comprehension and literary techniques, will be transferred to the books students read independently. Passive readers become active, avid readers.

SYNOPSIS

At Lincoln Elementary School, everyone knows Nick Allen, whose creative and unique ideas keep everybody on their toes. Nick meets his match when he walks into his language arts class on the first day of school. Mrs. Lorelei Granger, a veteran teacher, is both respected and feared by every fifth grader at Lincoln Elementary for her exacting standards—particularly in vocabulary.

The battle begins innocently enough on the first day of school when Nick finds that one of his classic stalling tactics earns him an extra report on the topic of word origins and the dictionary. Determined to gain the upper hand, he does a thorough job of researching the subject. When he attempts to use the report to stall the class again, he finds that Mrs. Granger sees through his ruse. Later that day with his dictionary report still fresh in his mind, Nick gets a brilliant idea for transforming into action Mrs. Granger's comment about the way words are created. Calling a pen a *frindle*, Nick soon convinces his friends to use the term. Everyone loves the new word Nick has coined, except Mrs. Granger. She is offended that a perfectly good word like *pen*, with its Latin origins, would be dropped in favor of *frindle* which she views as faddish nonsense. Determined to uphold standards, Mrs. Granger forbids the use of the word *frindle* in her classroom, which predictably results in its increased usage by students. Soon after the fracas begins, Mrs. Granger has an after-school conference with Nick. When it becomes clear that both are determined to hold their ground in the escalating feud, she gives him a sealed envelope and has him sign across the flap. She explains that its contents will be shared with Nick when the matter is finally resolved.

The word war heats up when Mrs. Granger's proscription against the use of *frindle* results in detention for over two hundred students. Once the local newspaper and then a network news program pick up the story, Nick is interviewed on national talk shows. While Nick remains respectful of Mrs. Granger during the publicity explosion, it becomes clear that her strong opposition to the use of the word and her determination to uphold the purity of the language have played a major role in turning a playful word game into a national craze. A local entrepreneur sees this as a marketing opportunity for frindles as well as related products, and he convinces Nick's father to sign a merchandising agreement in which a generous share of the profits will revert to a trust fund established in Nick's name.

The rest of the year passes, and the frindle-mania finally dies down, but the experience has had a sobering effect on Nick. His exuberance seems dampened, and he is careful to avoid becoming involved in anything controversial. He and Mrs. Granger part as friends at the end of fifth grade, and gradually over the summer he recovers his playful spirit and zest for life.

Years pass, and when Nick turns twenty-one, he finds that he is a very rich man due to the frindle trust fund. Soon afterward he receives a package from Mrs. Granger containing a new edition of *Webster's College Dictionary*, the mysterious envelope whose flap he had signed so many years ago, and Mrs. Granger's old fountain pen with the word *frindle* folded under its clip. In the dictionary he finds the entry for the word *frindle* with its origin attributed to him, and in the letter he finds an explanation of Mrs. Granger's actions so many years ago. He learns that her vigorous and public fight against the use of the word was actually a calculated strategy that she hoped would help promote acceptance of the word. That Christmas, Nick reciprocates by establishing a million-dollar scholarship fund in Mrs. Granger's name. He also sends her a beautiful gold fountain pen with instructions that she can call the object by any name she chooses.

PRE-READING ACTIVITIES

1. Preview the book by reading the title and author's name and by looking at the illustration on the cover. Have you ever heard the word *frindle*? What do you think it means? Check a dictionary to see if you can find the answer. What do you think the book *Frindle* will be about? Do you think the book will be humorous or serious? Have you read any other books by the same author?

2. In this book, a common object goes by several different names. Look at the following objects:

    Can you think of several different names for each object? How do you think these words came into being? Where could you look to find out?

3. The teacher in this story keeps her favorite book—a large unabridged dictionary—on a stand in the front of the room. To help you understand some of the words that she and the other characters use, you may want to keep a dictionary handy while reading this book. As a warm-up, look up the word "unabridged" and answer these questions:

    *   What are the guide words on the page where you found the word?

    *   How many syllables does the word have?

    *   What is its part of speech?

    *   What is the origin of the word?

4. One of the main characters in *Frindle* is a fifth-grader named Nick Allen who likes to liven up his days at school. Do you have any classmates who are pranksters or like to waste time in school?

5. Have you ever had a teacher who is fair but *very* strict? What are some of the advantages and disadvantages of this kind of teacher?

6. A fad is a craze or temporary fashion. Think of a time when someone in your school started a fad. In a small group, discuss how the fad started, how it spread, how long it lasted, and why it ended. Then ask your parents or older family members about fads that emerged when they were your age.

Pre-Reading Activities (cont.)

7. This book has a title for each chapter. Often a chapter title is a main idea, the name of a character, or a "catchy" phrase to capture the reader's interest. Scan the titles below. Based on these titles, write a sentence telling what you think each chapter might be about.

Chapter	Sentence
1. Nick	
2. Mrs. Granger	
3. The Question	
4. Word Detective	
5. The Report	
6. The Big Idea	
7. Word Wars	
8. Mightier than the Sword	
9. Chess	
10. Freedom of the Press	
11. Extra! Extra! Read All About It!	
12. Airwaves	
13. Ripples	
14. Inside Nick	
15. And the Winner Is . . .	

CHAPTERS 1 – 3

Vocabulary: Read each sentence. Use the context to help you figure out the meaning of the underlined word in each of the following sentences. Write your definition. Then compare your definition with a dictionary definition.

1. The teacher knew that announcing a surprise quiz would give the class a good <u>jolt</u> and make them pay attention.

   Your definition_____

   Dictionary definition _____

2. Mom <u>pounced</u> on Ben for carelessly leaving the screen door open and letting the cat escape.

   Your definition_____

   Dictionary definition _____

3. At the beginning of the year, most teachers carefully explain the class <u>procedures</u> and rules that they expect their students to follow.

   Your definition_____

   Dictionary definition _____

4. Asking granddad about his childhood is guaranteed to <u>launch</u> a series of amusing stories.

   Your definition_____

   Dictionary definition _____

5. The girl <u>hesitated</u> a moment to think before trying to spell the difficult word.

   Your definition_____

   Dictionary definition _____

> Read to find out what happens to Nick Allen on the first day of fifth grade.

Questions:

1. What had Nick done in the past to make life lively at Lincoln Elementary School?

2. Why isn't Nick pleased to be in Mrs. Granger's class?

3. How does Mrs. Granger share her interest in words with her students?

Chapters 1 – 3 (cont.)

4. Why does Mrs. Granger send a letter to the parents of every fifth grader? How do Nick and his mother each react to the letter?

5. Why does Nick ask Mrs. Granger about the origin of the words in a dictionary? How does she react to his question?

Questions for Discussion:

1. What do you think about Nick's behavior in school? Would you enjoy being his classmate? How would you feel about being his teacher?

2. Why do you think Mrs. Granger spends so much time on vocabulary work and the dictionary?

3. Do you think Mrs. Granger deserves her reputation for being a very tough teacher? What examples can you find in the text to prove your point?

Literary Device: Point of View

Point of view in a book of fiction refers to the person telling the story. Sometimes the author as narrator tells the story. Other times, the story is told by one of the story characters. Who is telling this story? How do you know?

_____

_____

_____

_____

_____

Writing Activity:

Nick's scheme for stalling the class backfired and now he has to prepare an extra report in addition to doing the regular homework. Write about a real or imagined experience of your own where a plan went wrong. What were the consequences?

Chapters 1 – 3 (cont.)

Literary Element: Characterization

In the chart below, list what you know about each important character you meet in the story. Add to this information as you continue to read the story. Add characters to the chart as you meet them in the story.

Character	Information
Nick Allen	
Mrs. Granger	
Mrs. Allen	
Mr. Allen	

CHAPTERS 4, 5

Vocabulary: Use the words in the Word Box and the clues below to complete the crossword puzzle.

WORD BOX
complex
fascinating
grumble
harsh
jammed
jumble
origins
primly
reputation
sidetrack

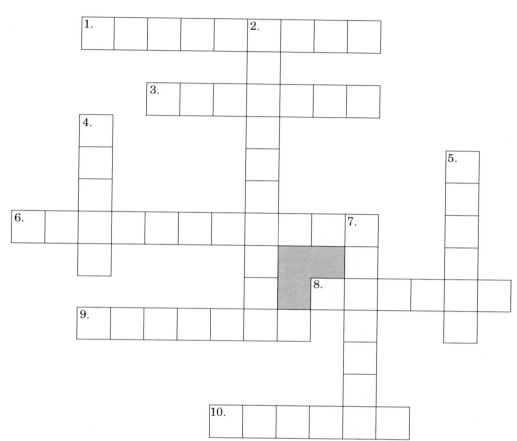

Across

1. turn aside from what is important

3. complicated

6. very interesting

8. disorganized collection

9. sources from which things come

10. filled tightly and completely

Down

2. opinion about one person held by others

4. unpleasant to any of the physical senses

5. very formally

7. complain

Read to find out how Nick turns his report for Mrs. Granger into something special.

Chapters 4, 5 (cont.)

Questions:

1. How does his family's homework rule affect Nick?
2. How does Nick prepare his report? What topics does it cover?
3. What is the difference between Phase One and Phase Two of Nick's report?
4. Why do Nick's classmates particularly enjoy Phase Two of Nick's report?
5. According to Mrs. Granger, how do words get their meanings, and when do new words enter the language?

Questions for Discussion:

1. What do you think of the "Homework First" rule? What are some advantages and disadvantages of this rule? How does this compare to the homework policy in your home?
2. What do you think of the way Mrs. Granger handles Nick's time-wasting schemes? Why do you think she does this?

Literary Element: Characterization

There is an old saying that the eyes are windows to a person's heart and mind. Reread Chapter Five looking for references to Mrs. Granger's eyes. Choose three references and think about what Mrs. Granger's eyes reveal about her feelings and thoughts. Record these observations in the following chart.

Page	Appearance of Mrs. Granger's Eyes	Meaning

Social Studies Connection:

In his oral report, Nick spoke about the work of Samuel Johnson, who was a famous English lexicographer (person who works on a dictionary). Go online to find information about Noah Webster who is considered to be the father of the American dictionary. What was his contribution and how has his work influenced the dictionaries we use today? Share your findings in either an oral or written report.

Chapters 4, 5 (cont.)

Dictionary Activities:

1. Read the etymology section in the front of a student dictionary to learn about words and their origins. In the space below, list important facts that Nick might have used in his report. One has been done for you. Compare your facts with those of your classmates.

Words and Their Origins

1. Many English words have been borrowed from other languages.

2. _____

_____

3. _____

_____

4. _____

_____

---

2. Look up the word "take" in your dictionary. How many different meanings does it have? Choose five definitions and write a sentence that illustrates each meaning. Read your sentences to a partner who should figure out the meaning in each of the sentences.

Writing Activity:

Imagine you are one of Nick's classmates. Write about Nick's behavior and your response to it on the day he read his report in class. Express your own opinion of Nick's classroom strategies and describe the way Mrs. Granger reacts.

CHAPTERS 6 – 8

Vocabulary: Draw a line from each word on the left to its definition on the right. Then use the numbered words to fill in the blanks in the sentences below.

	A		B
1.	concentration	a.	solemn swearing to keep a promise
2.	clattered	b.	punishment of keeping students after school
3.	oath	c.	close attention
4.	detention	d.	strange; odd
5.	weird	e.	made a loud rattling noise

. . . .

1. Students who misbehave in class may receive _____.

2. Tom thought it was _____ to see the small cat chase the large dog.

3. I study in the library so that nothing will disturb my _____.

4. Before becoming president of the club, Jane raised her right hand and repeated the _____ of office.

5. The metal pans banged and _____ when Paul put them away in the cupboard.

> Read to find out about Nick's big idea.

Questions:

1. What is Nick's big idea? What gave him this idea?

2. How does Nick begin to put his plan into action?

3. How does Nick launch the new word at school?

4. Why doesn't Mrs. Granger approve of Nick's new word? Why do her attempts to ban the word fail?

5. Why does Mrs. Granger insist that Nick sign and date an envelope during their conference?

Chapters 6 – 8 (cont.)

Questions for Discussion:

1. Why do you think the author includes the story about the *gwagala*?

2. Why do you think Mrs. Granger reacts intensely to Nick's new word?

3. Imagine yourself as a classmate of Nick's. What would you have done during the class picture? Would you have dared to ask Mrs. Granger for a frindle?

4. What do you think Mrs. Granger has written in the letter she placed inside the sealed envelope?

Literary Devices:

I. *Allusion*—An allusion is a reference in literature to a familiar person, place, object, event, or saying. The title of Chapter Eight, "Mightier than the Sword," is an allusion to the famous saying "The pen is mightier than the sword." This means that the power of words is often much stronger than the power of physical force. Keeping this allusion in mind, reread Chapter Eight. Then tell how this quotation relates to the content of this chapter.

_____

_____

II. *Simile*—A simile is a figure of speech in which two unlike objects are compared using the words "like" or "as." For example:

> Nick was excited. It [his after-school meeting with Mrs. Granger] was kind of like a conference during a war. One side waves a white flag, and the generals come out and talk. General Nicholas Allen. Nick liked the sound of it.

What is being compared?

_____

What is the effect of this comparison?

_____

_____

Writing Activity:

Based on what you have read so far, write a letter from Mrs. Granger to Nick. Place this letter in an envelope and seal it, and then sign across the flap just as Mrs. Granger asked Nick to do. Put the envelope in a safe place and don't open it until Nick receives Mrs. Granger's letter later in the book.

CHAPTERS 9 – 11

Vocabulary: Antonyms are words with opposite meanings. Draw a line from each word in column A to its antonym in column B. Then use the words in column A to fill in the blanks in the sentences below.

	A		B
1.	rowdy	a.	forbidding
2.	disrespectful	b.	contented
3.	encouraging	c.	orderly
4.	annoyed	d.	genuine
5.	phony	e.	courteous

. . . .

1. Speaking rudely to a teacher is an example of _____ behavior.

2. The diamond looked so real that only a jeweler could tell that it was a(n) _____.

3. Mother becomes _____ when one of us is late for dinner.

4. The cheers and whistles from the _____ crowd made it impossible to hear the speaker.

5. Dad gave us a(n) _____ smile and told us that even though the hill was steep, he was sure we could make it to the top.

Read to find out what happens when the principal comes to visit Mr. and Mrs. Allen.

Questions:

1. Why does Mrs. Chatham visit the Allens' home?

2. How do Mr. and Mrs. Allen each feel about Mrs. Chatham's complaint?

3. Why doesn't Nick think he can stop his friends from using the word "frindle"?

4. Why does Judy Morgan visit Lincoln Elementary School?

5. Why doesn't Nick reveal his identity to Judy Morgan?

6. How do the school superintendent and Mrs. Granger react to Judy Morgan's news article?

Chapters 9 – 11 (cont.)

Questions for Discussion:

1. Were you surprised by Mr. and Mrs. Allen's reaction to Mrs. Chatham's visit? How do you think most parents would react in the same situation?

2. Why do you think Judy Morgan wants to talk to everyone before writing her story? Do you think her article is fair?

Literary Devices:

I. *Metaphor*—A metaphor is a figure of speech in which two unlike objects are compared. Unlike a simile, a metaphor does not use the words "as" or "like" to make the comparison. For example:

> It was a chess game, Nick against Mrs. Granger. Mrs. Granger had just tried to end the game by using her queen—Mrs. Chatham in her black raincoat, the black queen.

> Nick didn't know it until the attack was under way, but he had a powerful defender of his own—good old Mom, the white queen.

What is the controversy over the word *frindle* being compared to?

_____

What are Mrs. Chatham and Mrs. Allen each being compared to?

_____

_____

II. *Allusion*—In the headline of her newspaper article, Judy Morgan makes an allusion to Noah Webster. Review the research you did on Noah Webster for the Social Studies Connection on page eight of this study guide. What do you think Judy Morgan meant when she said, "Move over, Mr. Webster," in the headline of her article?

_____

_____

_____

_____

Chapters 9 – 11 (cont.)

Literary Element: Conflict

A conflict in a story is a clash between opposing forces. Fill in the chart below with examples of the conflicts that appear in the book.

Conflict	Example
Nick *vs.* Mrs. Granger	
Mrs. Granger *vs.* the fifth grade	
Mrs. Chatham *vs.* Mrs. Allen	
Superintendent *vs.* Mrs. Chatham	

Writing Activity:

Reread the excerpts from Judy Morgan's article that appear in Chapter Eleven. Then use what you know about the word war that is going on between Nick and Mrs. Granger to write your own news article about the events at Lincoln Elementary School. In writing your article, remember to include answers to these key questions: *Who? What? When? Where? Why?* and *How?*

CHAPTER 12

Vocabulary: Read each group of words. Choose the one word or phrase that does not belong with the others and cross it out. On the line below the words, tell how the rest of the words are alike.

1. flood   tornado   shower   earthquake

   These words are alike because _____.

2. official   lights   cameras   microphones

   These words are alike because _____.

3. contract   videotape   royalty   trademark

   These words are alike because _____.

4. deposit   trust account   check   professor

   These words are alike because _____.

5. reporter   principal   producer   anchorman

   These words are alike because _____.

> Read to find out what happens as a result of the article in *The Westfield Gazette.*

Questions:

1. What price does Nick pay for being famous?
2. How does the frindle story become national news?
3. Why is Mrs. Allen worried about Nick's interview?
4. What happens as a result of all the publicity?
5. What deal does Bud Lawrence work out with Mr. Allen?

Questions for Discussion:

1. Why do you think so many people are interested in the frindle story?
2. Imagine Nick as a guest on a television talk show. What do you think Nick and the host would talk about? What jokes might the host tell about the frindle? What advice would you give Nick before he goes on the show?
3. In your opinion, should Bud Lawrence be making a deal with Mr. Allen? If you were Mr. Allen, would you sign the contract?

Chapter 12 (cont.)

Language Study: Idioms

An idiom is an expression that doesn't mean what the words actually say. For example, when Mrs. Allen tells Nick "to mind his Ps and Qs" during the interview with Alice Lunderson, she is not really telling him to think about these letters. Instead she is warning him to _____

_____

Do some research to find out the origin of the expression "to mind your Ps and Qs." Like Nick, you can share your findings in an oral report.

Art Connection:

Imagine that Mr. Lawrence has just hired you to design the latest frindle T-shirt. Printers in Massachusetts, Chicago, and Los Angles are all waiting for a design. Make copies of the sirt below. Sketch your design for the front and back of your shirt. You might want to enlarge your design and use fabric crayons to transfer your design to a plain cotton T-shirt.

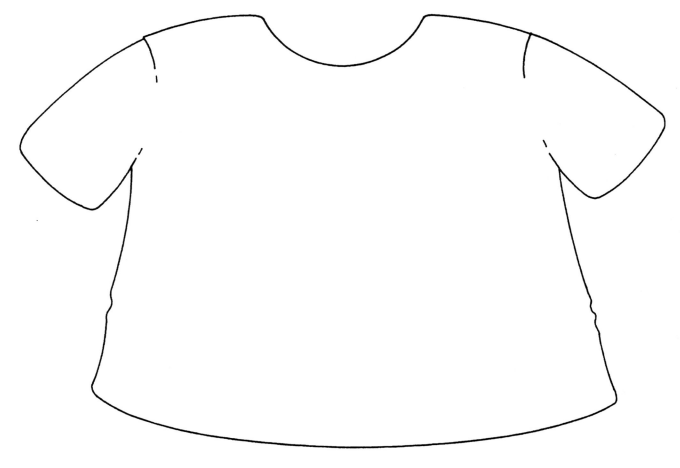

Chapter 12 (cont.)

Math Connection:

Mr. Lawrence and Mr. Allen agree that Mr. Lawrence will give Nick a thirty percent royalty on any profits made from selling products related to frindles. Begin by calculating the total profit on the sale of each item shown below in the chart. Finally, find the total royalty payment and fill out the check with this amount. Remember that on a check, the amount is written in numbers and also in words.

Item	Number Sold	Profit Per Item	Total Profit	30% Royalty
Ballpoint Pens	146,400	$.10	$14,640.00	$4,392.00
T-shirts	15,900	$2.75		
Sweatshirts	9,400	$6.00		
Notebooks	55,650	$.40		

Total Royalty = _____

	1 2 3 4 5
DOLLARS BANK	DATE _____
	$ [ ]
PAY TO THE ORDER OF _____	
_____	_____
_____	_____

Writing Activity:

Alice Lunderson had a challenging job to fit all of her interview into just two minutes of air time. Write a script of her news feature. You will need to include comments by Nick, Mrs. Allen, Mrs. Granger, Mrs. Chatham, and Mr. Lawrence. Read your script aloud and time how long it takes. Keep cutting it until it is exactly two minutes long. Once it is the correct length of time, ask some classmates to help you make a video or an audiotape of the interview.

CHAPTERS 13 – 15

Vocabulary: Analogies are equations in which the first pair of words has the same relationship as the second pair of words. For example: KITTEN is to CAT as PUPPY is to DOG. Both word parts name baby animals and the adult animals they become. Decide which word best completes each word analogy and write it in the blank.

1. BANK ROBBER is to CRIMINAL as MOVIE STAR is to _____.

   a. musician   b. celebrity   c. writer   d. dancer

2. GOOD is to EVIL as HERO is to _____.

   a. villain   b. drama   c. sandwich   d. star

3. SELL is to MERCHANT as BUY is to _____.

   a. rascal   b. coinage   c. consumer   d. advocate

4. BALL is to ROUND as SHOEBOX is to _____.

   a. oval   b. oblong   c. square   d. spherical

5. LETTERS is to CORRESPONDENCE as CONTRIBUTION is to _____.

   a. taxation   b. trust fund   c. scholarship   d. donation

> Read to find out what happens to Nick as he grows up.

Questions:

1. What impact does the word *frindle* have on Westfield? What impact does it have on the rest of the country?

2. How does Nick change as a result of his experience with the word *frindle*?

3. Why does Nick visit Mrs. Granger's classroom on the last day of school? What does she say about the envelope? What advice does she give Nick?

4. How does Nick's life change when he turns twenty-one?

5. What does Nick learn when he finally opens the envelope?

6. How does Nick honor Mrs. Granger?

Chapters 13 – 15 (cont.)

Questions for Discussion:

1. In your opinion, does Nick use his money wisely?
2. What do you think Mrs. Granger means when she says she chose to play the villain in the frindle drama? Why do you think she chose this role? What might have happened if she had not strongly objected to the word?
3. Do you agree with Mrs. Granger about the importance of words and the dictionary?

Graphic Organizer:

Pretend that you have just been hired by Bud Lawrence to find new product ideas for frindle-related items. Add your ideas to the list of items already in production. Draw a star next to the product that you think will make the most money. Then tell a partner why you feel as you do.

Frindle Product Line	
1. frindle ballpoints	6._____
2. frindle shirts	7._____
3. frindle sunglasses	8._____
4. frindle erasers	9._____
5. frindle notebooks	10._____

Literary Devices:

I. *Symbolism*—A symbol in literature refers to an object, a person, or an event that represents an idea or a set of ideas.

What do you think Mrs. Granger's old maroon fountain pen symbolized?

_____

What do you think the new gold frindle Nick gave Mrs. Granger symbolized?

_____

II. *Irony*—Irony refers to a situation that turns out to be the opposite of what is expected. What is ironic about Mrs. Granger's letter to Nick?

_____

Chapters 13 – 15 (cont.)

Word Study:

As Nick discovered, the English language is constantly changing. Words such as *pen* and *ice box* are being replaced by words like *refrigerator* and *frindle*. Think about the words in the two columns below. Use a dictionary to find out what each word means. Think of several more new words that have entered our language in the past few years, and then share your words with a partner.

Old Words	New Words
emporium –	video –
reticule –	cyberspace –
snood –	computer –

Writing Activity:

Nick and Mrs. Granger are both very surprised and pleased by the gifts they receive from each other. Imagine you are Nick or Mrs. Granger and write a thank-you letter. It should have the same form as a friendly letter. Be sure to include a return address and date, a greeting, the body of the letter, the closing, and the signature. Before making a final copy, be sure to proofread your letter for spelling and punctuation.

CLOZE ACTIVITY

The following passage has been taken from Chapter Thirteen of the book. Read the entire passage before filling in the blanks. Then reread the passage and fill in each blank with a word that makes sense. Finally, you may compare your words with those of the author.

But life did settle back to normal in Westfield. More leaves fell, Thanksgiving came, _____[1] the first snow, then Christmas, and more _____.[2] Fall and winter seemed to calm everything _____[3] and drive everyone into their own houses.

_____[4] were calmer at Lincoln Elementary School, too. _____[5] was over. But that didn't mean the _____[6] was gone. Not at all.

All the _____[7] and even some of the teachers used _____[8] new word. At first it was on _____.[9] Then it became a habit, and by _____[10] middle of February, *frindle* was just a _____,[11] like *door* or *tree* or *hat*. People _____[12] Westfield barely noticed it anymore.

But in _____[13] rest of the country, things were hopping. _____[14] was on the move. In hundreds of _____[15] towns and big cities from coast to _____,[16] kids were using the new word, and _____[17] and teachers were trying to stop it. _____[18] had happened in Westfield happened over and _____[19] and over again.

Bud Lawrence couldn't have _____[20] happier. There were frindle shirts and sunglasses _____[21] erasers and notebooks and paper and dozens _____[22] other items. The new line of frindles _____[23] from Japan were a big hit, and _____[24] there was talk of selling them in _____[25] and Europe, as well. The checks that _____[26] into Nick's trust fund got bigger and _____.[27]

Bud opened his own factory in Westfield _____[28] make frindle baseball caps, which created jobs _____[29] twenty-two people. And in March the town _____[30] voted to put up a little sign _____[31] the post below the town's name along _____[32] 302. It said, "Home of the Original Frindle."

POST-READING ACTIVITIES

1. Return to the chart of chapter titles that you began in the Pre-Reading Activities on page three of this study guide. Were any of your guesses about the content of the chapters correct?

2. Return to the character chart that you began on page six of this study guide. Add character names and information about the characters. Share your responses with those of your classmates.

3. Try launching a new word just as Nick had done. Once you have invented the word and established its definition, plan a way to get people to use the word. To determine if your word is adopted, keep a log of the number of times you hear people using the word. After several days, write a summary telling what happened to your word. Based on your experience, share any ideas that you have on why a made-up word is either a short-term fad or a long-term success.

4. The students in Mrs. Granger's class learned about many types of dictionaries. Visit your local public library and look at the different dictionaries in the reference section. How many different kinds of dictionaries can you find? When would you use each type of dictionary? Look up the word "pen" in a student dictionary, a collegiate dictionary, an unabridged dictionary, and a foreign dictionary. How do the definitions differ?

5. As Nick learned when he did his report on dictionaries, the origin of a word is called its etymology. Mrs. Granger explained the etymology of the word "pen" by saying that it came from the Latin word *pinna*, which means feather. Many dictionaries include an entry word's etymology at the beginning or at the end of the definition. In addition, there are specialized dictionaries such as *Webster's Dictionary of Word Origins* and *The Barnhart Dictionary of Etymology* that deal specifically with word origins. Use a dictionary to find the etymology of each of the words listed in the box below. Then share and discuss your findings.

history	photographer	superintendent	principal

6. How would you rate the book *Frindle*? Write a one-page book review. Google the following keywords to see how others have reviewed the book: online book review *Frindle*. Display your review on a bulletin board in your classroom.

7. Designate a spot on the chalkboard or on a bulletin board for a class "word for the day." Then take turns with your classmates posting an interesting new word each morning. During the day, find time to look up the word to discover its pronunciation and its meaning. Record this information in a special section of your notebook. Try to share what you have learned about the word with a partner. Learning just one new word each day will do wonders for your vocabulary.

Post-Reading Activities (cont.)

8. One of the most famous poems that uses made-up nonsense words is "Jabberwocky" by Lewis Carroll. This poem, which can be found in many anthologies, including *The Random House Book of Poetry*, first appeared in Carroll's classic children's book *Through the Looking Glass*. Find a copy of the poem and read it. Then choose at least five made-up words from the poem and create definitions for these words. Use the positions of the words in the sentences as well as the meaning of surrounding words to help you determine your definitions. Then try writing your own poem with made-up words. Share both your poem and its "translation" with others.

9. Soon after its publication, *Frindle* received the Christopher Award, which is awarded to books that "affirm the highest values of the human spirit." Pretend that you are on the award committee. Write a speech in which you explain whether or not you think this book should receive the award. Use examples from the text to support your position.

10. Try to picture the scene at Nick's twenty-first birthday when his parents tell him about the trust fund, and Nick learns that he is a multi-millionaire. Imagine that this happened to you. What would you do for your family members? What would you do for yourself? How would you give away a million dollars?

11. **Readers Theater:** Read a chapter of the book as though it were a play. Choose a chapter, such as Chapter Six, that has a lot of dialogue and has two or more characters in conversation. Select a classmate to read each role and then select another to read the narration. The characters should read only those words inside the quotation marks. Ignore phrases such as "he said" or "she said." You may want to use simple props, such as hats, to identify characters or small objects to identify the setting.

12. **Literature Circle:** Have a literature circle discussion in which you tell your personal reactions to *Frindle*. Here are some questions and sentence starters to help your literature circle begin a discussion.

   • How are you like Nick? How are you different?
   • Do you find the characters in the book realistic? Why or why not?
   • Which character did you like the most? The least?
   • Who else would you like to read this book? Why?
   • What questions would you like to ask the author about this book?
   • It was not fair when . . .
   • I would have like to see . . .
   • I wonder . . .
   • Nick learned that . . .

SUGGESTIONS FOR FURTHER READING

Beal, George. *The Kingfisher Book of Words*. Kingfisher Books.

Christensen, Bonnie. *Rebus Riot*. Scholastic.

Cole, Joanna, and Stephanie Calmenson, eds. *Six Sick Sheep: 101 Tongue Twisters*. Scholastic.

* DeGross, Monalisa. *Donovan's Word Jar*. HarperCollins.

Heller, Ruth. *Many Luscious Lollipops: A Book About Adjectives*. Puffin.

——————. *Merry-Go-Round: A Book About Nouns*. Puffin.

——————. *Up, Up and Away: A Book About Adverbs*. Puffin.

Juster, Norton. *As: A Surfeit of Similes*. HarperCollins.

* ——————. *The Phantom Tollbooth*. Knopf.

McMillan, Bruce, and Brett McMillan. *Puniddles*. Sandpiper.

Most, Bernard. *Hippopotamus Hunt*. Harcourt.

Schwartz, Alvin. *A Twister of Twists, A Tangler of Tongues*. HarperCollins.

Terban, Marvin. *The Dove Dove: Funny Homograph Riddles*. Sandpiper.

——————. *Eight Ate: A Feast of Homonym Riddles*. Sandpiper.

——————. *Guppies in Tuxedos: Funny Eponyms*. Sandpiper.

——————. *I Think I Thought and Other Tricky Verbs*. Sandpiper.

——————. *In a Pickle and Other Funny Idioms*. Sandpiper.

——————. *Mad as a Wet Hen! And Other Funny Idioms*. Sandpiper.

——————. *Superdupers! Really Funny Words*. Sandpiper.

——————. *Too Hot to Hoot: Funny Palindrome Riddles*. Sandpiper.

——————. *Your Foot's on My Feet! And Other Tricky Nouns*. Sandpiper.

Van Allsburg, Chris. *The Z was Zapped: A Play in Twenty-Six Acts*. Sandpiper.

* NOVEL-TIES study guides are available for these titles.

ANSWER KEY

Chapters 1 – 3
Vocabulary:
1. jolt–abrupt surprise or shock   2. pounced–scolded or reprimanded   3. procedures–set ways to act or do things   4. launch–start something with enthusiasm   5. hesitated–paused

Questions:
1. To make things lively at Lincoln Elementary during his third-grade year, Nick convinced his classmates to turn their classroom into a tropical island. In fourth grade, he and a friend made bird-like chirps to annoy the teacher. 2. Nick is not pleased to be in Mrs. Granger's class because she is reputed to be a very strict teacher with X-ray vision who unfailingly catches students who misbehave. 3. Mrs. Granger shares her love of words and the dictionary with her class by having a "Word for the Day" that every student must research and learn. She also has weekly vocabulary tests. 4. Mrs. Granger sends a letter to parents explaining that every student must have a dictionary for home study. In her letter she provides a list of acceptable dictionaries. Nick's mother thinks the letter is wonderful and says that Mrs. Granger is a very dedicated teacher. Nick thinks it is going to be a difficult year. 5. Nick asks Mrs. Granger about the origin of the words in a dictionary as a stalling strategy so Mrs. Granger won't have time to give homework. Mrs. Granger responds by assigning Nick an oral report on the subject due the next day.

Chapters 4, 5
Vocabulary:
Across–1. sidetrack   3. complex   6. fascinating   8. jumble   9. origins   10. jammed; Down–2. reputation   4. harsh   5. primly   7. grumble

Questions:
1. Because Nick's family has the "Homework First" rule, meaning that homework must be done right after school before any leisure time activities, Nick cannot play baseball with the other boys until he does his homework for Mrs. Granger. 2. To prepare his report, Nick looks in the front of his dictionary for information on word origins. Then he checks two encyclopedias and reads what each says under the entry *Dictionary*. After reading this information, he makes notes about what he will talk about in his oral report. The topics he covers are: the first English dictionary, the growth of the English language, William Shakespeare, words from French and German, new words, old words, new inventions, Anglo-Saxon words, Latin and Greek roots, and American English. 3. In Phase One, Nick talks from his own notes. In Phase Two, Nick reads a long excerpt from an article on word origins that he found in his dictionary. 4. Nick's classmates prefer Phase Two because they realize that he is doing this to waste classroom time and to avoid doing the work that Mrs. Granger had planned for the class. 5. Mrs. Granger says that words get their meanings from what people have determined their meanings to be. Usage determines the words that go into the dictionary and how they are defined. New words enter the language when there is a need for them.

Chapters 6 – 8
Vocabulary:
1. c   2. e   3. a   4. b   5. d; 1. detention   2. weird   3. concentration   4. oath   5. clattered
Questions:
1. Nick's big idea is to invent the word "frindle" and see if he can get people to use it in place of the word "pen." Three things lead to his big idea: first, Janet finds a pen; second, Nick realizes the meaning of what Mrs. Granger has said about word meanings and where they come from by thinking of an instance in his own life when he created a word; third, the nonsense word *frindle* comes to mind when he hands Janet a pen she has dropped. 2. To put his plan into action, Nick buys a pen at the Penny Pantry and calls it "frindle." He has several friends do the same thing. Then Nick and these friends sign an oath to promote the use of the word "frindle" in place of the word "pen." 3. Nick launches the new word in Mrs. Granger's language arts class. He pretends to have forgotten his pen, which he calls a "frindle." His friend tosses him a frindle which Nick drops. During this exchange, they use the word "frindle" many times. 4. Mrs. Granger disapproves of the word "frindle" because the word "pen" has a perfectly good history and a Latin origin. She tries to stop the children from using the new word by assigning those who use it to detention. There they must write a punishment exercise. It doesn't work because the more Mrs. Granger forbids the word, the more students want to use it. 5. During their conference, Mrs. Granger shows Nick an envelope. She makes him sign and date the back so that when he finally opens the letter, he will know that she has not made any changes to the letter's contents. She plans to give it to Nick when the disagreement over the word "frindle" is finally over.

Chapters 9 – 11

Vocabulary:
Questions:

1. c 2. e 3. a 4. b 5. d; 1. disrespectful 2. phony 3. annoyed 4. rowdy 5. encouraging
1. Mrs. Chatham, the principal of Lincoln Elementary School, speaks to Nick and his parents about the disruption the word "frindle" is causing at school. She is upset because Nick and the rest of the students are showing disrespect when they defy her ban on the new word. 2. Mrs. Allen does not see the harm in what is happening as long Nick is not being disrespectful. She feels that the adults at the school are overreacting to a harmless experiment with language. Mr. Allen is not so sure. While he says that it is not a malicious prank, he does understand that the new word is causing a great disruption. 3. Nick doesn't think he can stop his friends from using the word "frindle" because the word no longer belongs to him. It has become a real word now because people are using it. 4. Judy Morgan is a newspaper reporter who visits the school because it has been rumored that there have been mass detentions and that there is a secret code word being used at the school. 5. Nick realizes that if he reveals his identity to Judy Morgan, he might inadvertently say something that she would put in her article that would get him into trouble. 6. The school superintendent is angry at the principal because he thinks the article is bad publicity for the school district. Mrs. Chatham is angry at Mrs. Granger for what she said to the reporter.

Chapter 12

Vocabulary:

1. shower–the other words are alike because they all name natural disasters 2. official–the other words are alike because they all name equipment that is used in producing a television show or film 3. videotape–the other words are alike because they all have to do with legal issues concerning the ownership of property 4. professor–the other words are alike because they all have to do with banking 5. principal–the other words are alike because they all name roles of people who work with news media

Questions:

1. As a consequence of his fame, Nick has lost his privacy: he is noticed wherever he goes. His classmates always expect him to be clever and funny, while adults expect him to do something that will cause another problem at school. 2. Judy Morgan's story is read by Alice Lunderson, a part-time employee at a local TV station. She tells the station manager who then calls the Boston CBS station. The woman in Boston thinks it is such a good story that she calls the network news editor in New York. Alice then arranges to interview people in Westfield and the story appears on the national evening news as a closing story. 3. Mrs. Allen is worried about Nick's interview because she thinks he may say something embarrassing for the family, for the school, or for the town. 4. As other TV news and entertainment shows pick up the story, the word *frindle* begins to spread across the country as other children hear and use the word. 5. Bud Lawrence, a local businessman, sees the potential for selling products connected to the word *frindle*. He agrees to put 30% of all profits in a trust fund in Nick's name in exchange for the right to use the word.

Chapters 13 – 15

Vocabulary:
Questions:

1. b–celebrity 2. a–villain 3. c–consumer 4. b–oblong 5. d–donation
1. The word *frindle* becomes a habit and people begin to use it all the time. Mr. Lawrence opens a hat factory in Westfield that employs twenty-two people. A sign marking Westfield as the home of the frindle is erected on the road into town. As the word *frindle* sweeps the country, parents and teachers object to the word, and children want to use it. People buy lots of frindle-related products. 2. As a result of his experience with the word *frindle*, Nick becomes much more cautious and quiet for the rest of fifth grade, not wanting to do anything else to call attention to himself. 3. Nick visits Mrs. Granger's class on the last day of school to pick up the envelope that he signed in the fall. She says that the frindle matter is not yet over and that she will mail him the envelope when it is finally resolved. She tells Nick not to be upset or deterred by what happened. She expresses her confidence in him and says that she expects him to do great things. 4. When he turns twenty-one, Nick learns about the trust fund which has made him very wealthy. Nick gives money to his parents so they can travel and to his brother so he can educate his child. He buys a fancy mountain bike and a new computer for himself. 5. From the letter in the envelope, Nick learns that Mrs. Granger's opposition to the word *frindle* stemmed from a desire to help promote the word by drawing attention to it. 6. Nick honors Mrs. Granger by establishing a million-dollar scholarship fund in her name. He also gives her a gold pen with an inscription saying that she can call the pen by any name she chooses.